AF228215

MATTAPAN
THROUGH TIME

ANTHONY M. SAMMARCO

CONTEMPORARY PHOTOGRAPHS BY PETER B. KINGMAN

AMERICA
THROUGH
TIME

This book is dedicated to the late Robert M. Cohen

ראבערט כהן איז געווען א פיינער, אויפשטייגערער איד און דאס בוך איז אים געווידמעט

AMERICA THROUGH TIME®
An imprint of SUTTON PUBLISHING INC.
www.through-time.com

First published 2023
Reprinted 2025

Copyright © Anthony M. Sammarco 2023, 2025

ISBN 978-1-63499-451-4

All rights reserved. No part of this publication may be reproduced, stored in a retrieval system or transmitted in any form or by any means, electronic, mechanical, photocopying, recording or otherwise, without prior permission in writing from Sutton Publishing Inc.

Typeset in Mrs Eaves XL Serif Narrow
Printed and bound in the United States of America by Integrated Books International

CONTENTS

A Type Four streetcar travels south on Blue Hill Avenue as it passes the famous Oriental Theatre, which was designed by Krokyn, Browne & Rosenstein. Opened in 1930, the theater had a magical ceiling of twinkling stars and moving clouds. The Chinese-themed exterior and interior emulated such notable Chinese structures as the Street Gate of Tsinanfu and the façade of the Wan Shou Tsu Temple, in addition to a monumental vertical neon sign on the façade. On the right is the spire of St. Angela Merici Church, now Our Lady of Mount Carmel Parish. (Courtesy Frank Cheney)

Acknowledgments

I wish to especially thank Peter Bryant Kingman for his wonderful contemporary photographs of Mattapan. He has captured the essence of the vintage photographs and has made this book not just an interesting compilation of the houses, businesses, squares and streetscapes of this historic neighborhood of Boston, but a visually fascinating one as well

I also want to thank Jeff Rubin for his insights and suggestions on this book. He created the Facebook page "Dorchester-Mattapan-Randolph for Those Born in the 1950s" for people to reconnect and reestablished a sense of community.

We wish to extend my sincere thanks and deep appreciation to: Rona Alex; Joel Andreasen; Harvey Avidon; Frank Bernstein; The Blue Hill Avenue Kibbitzers Facebook Page; Andrea Soleil Parad Bornstein; Boston City Archives; Boston Public Library, David Leonard; Boston University School of Theology Library, Kara Jackman; Harriet Goldman Burak; Mary Jo Campbell; Mary Ellen Carney; the late Hutchinson Cedmarco; Pasqualina and Danny Cedmarco; Cesidio "Joe" Cedrone; Church of the Holy Spirit, Rev. Zenetta M. Armstrong; the late Frank Cheney; Wesley Chused, Esq.; City of Boston, ISD, Brigid Kenny-White; Edie Clifford; Harriet Slavin Cohen; Ronnie Cohen; Jim Coleman, Jr.; Colortek, Jackie Anderson; Arthur Cote, Jr.; Dandler Family Archives; Davis Square Architects; John R. Delaney; Robin Dexter; Digital Commonwealth; Dorchester-Mattapan-Randolph Facebook Page; Barbara Duby; eBay; Mary Ann English; the late Jorge and Ida Pearles Epstein; Leonard Federico; Maureen Ferris; Claire Finn; Dorothy Fleming; Shirley Frank; Rhonda Schwartz Friedman; Ron Garvey; Allan Gellerman; George Gershman; Howard M. Glassman; Ethel Cohen Goodrich; Edward Gordon; Helen Hannon; Lawrence Harmon; Diane Davidson Jacobs; Aaron Johnson; George Kalchev, Fonthill Media; Bill Kass; the late Rosamond and Aimee Lamb; Hillel Levine; Burt Lewis and Family; Joe Libeskind; Mattapan Branch, Boston Public Library, Maurice J. Gordon; Mattapan Square Main Streets, Nicole Echemendia, president; Richard McEvoy; Paul McKeen; Scott Miller; Mateusz Minsky; Norman Morris, author *Ghetto Memories*; Joe Moscaritolo; Frank Norton; James O'Keefe; Orleans Camera; Mark Ozer; Steven Pagatch; Parkway United Methodist Church, Rev. Tom Getchell Lacey, and Carla Ganter, Church Administrator; Presbyterian Historical Society, Sharon Reid; Linda Zweigman Pearl; Lilian M.C. Randall; Susan Cote Romanski; the late Francis Hamburger Russell; Joan Rutstein; Dennis Ryan; Jeffrey Salloway; Mindy Sanderson; Bob Sawtelle; Rebecca Scimone; Ron Scully; Jeff Silver; Maureen Smith; Alan Sutton, Fonthill Media; Jamie Sutton; Schlossberg Memorial Chapel, Kenneth and Ilyana Schlossberg; Rebecca Scimone; Jeff Silver; Kena Longabaugh Smith; Bruce Spellman; Joan Stern; Jim Sullivan; Alan Sutton, Fonthill Media; Jamie Sutton; the late Paul Trusten; Kenneth Turino and Chris Matthias; Archives and Special Collections, University of Massachusetts, Sammarco Collection; Barbara Sweeney Valente; Victory Christian Assembly of God, Rev. Christo A Kamara; Ben Visnick; Martin Visnick; Wellfleet Historical Society, David Wright, Curator; Daniel White; Stacie Cohen Withington; The Wyner Family Jewish Heritage Center at New England Historic Genealogical Society, Lindsay Sprechman Murphy, Senior Archivist; Rich Zides.

INTRODUCTION

The name Mattapan originated with the Neponset Tribe of the Massachusett Indians, the original inhabitants of Mattapan, who were a tribe of the Massachusetts confederation of Native Americans. From the earliest settlement by the Puritans arriving in 1630 on the ship *Mary and John* from England seeking religious freedom, Dorchester was to become one of the largest towns in 17th century Massachusetts Bay Colony. At one time it included present day South Boston, Squantum, Hyde Park, Milton, Canton, Foxboro, Wrentham, Sharon, Stoughton, Raynham as well as *Mattapanock*, the Native American name for Mattapan. The word is loosely translated as meaning *"A Sitting down place"* but others have suggested that the word has an evil or sinister connotation, referring to an epidemic that in 1617 decimated a number Native Americans in the area, after which the survivors dubbed it Mattapanock, or *"Evil spread about the place."*

In the 17th and 18th centuries, the area now referred to as Mattapan, was primarily open lands with roads such as Norfolk Street, a trail that led to Dedham, and River Street which paralleled the Neponset River. *Unquityquisset*, the term for Upper Falls, referred to the dam that provided water power for the paper mill opened by James Boise and Hugh McLean in 1728. At this time, small scale industrial development began along the Neponset River, and the water power would spur on additional mills at the Upper Falls as well as *Unquety*, the Lower Falls at Dorchester Lower Mills. In fact, water power allowed the operation of the first grist mill in New England opened by Israel Stoughton in 1634, the first gun powder mill in 1678, the first paper mill in 1728 and the first chocolate mill in 1765.

Mattapan began to evolve as a neighborhood when the Brush Hill Turnpike was built in 1809 from Dudley Street in Roxbury to Mattapan Square. This toll road allowed wagons and carts to bring produce and goods into Boston on a fairly smooth and flat roadbed, but an act was passed in 1810 prohibiting the "Brush Hill Turnpike from collecting toll from anyone on military duty, on religious duty, coming to or from any grist mill, or on the common or ordinary business of family concerns, or from anyone who had not been out of town with a loaded team or carriage." Nonetheless as the surrounding streets such as River, Norfolk, Washington and Adams Streets in Dorchester were free of tolls, the turnpike eventually failed and in 1870 became a public highway and was renamed Blue Hill Avenue. In 1847 the Dorchester and Milton Branch of the Old Colony Railroad was extended from Ashmont in Dorchester to Mattapan Square and provided train service into downtown Boston at Kneeland Street. With the New York, New Haven and Hartford Railroad, which merged with the Old Colony Railroad in 1893, passenger stations *Rugby* on Randolph Road, *Mattapan* at Blue Hill Avenue and Norfolk (now Babson) Street and *Forest Avenue* at Morton Street allowed commuters to live in the newly developing "Streetcar Suburb" neighborhood until discontinued in 1944. Eventually, electric streetcars replaced horse drawn streetcars and serviced Blue Hill Avenue; by 1906 streetcars connected Mattapan Square to Egleston Square in Roxbury on the Boston Elevated Railway.

By the turn of the 20th century, Mattapan began to see the development of new streets laid out off Blue Hill Avenue and Norfolk Street which slowly become a solid, respectable suburb. Though predominantly Yankee in the late 19th century, within a decade or two the area began to attract new residents with diverse ethnic and religious backgrounds. Francis Hamburger Russell, who was raised on Wellington Hill in Mattapan, wrote in the chapter "The Hill, the Hollow, and the Jews" in his book *The Great Interlude* said "The Irish would drive out the old Yankees, as they did from the handsome swell-fronted town houses of Charlestown, The Poles, although religiously akin, nevertheless replaced the Irish rather than mingle with them. The Jews displaced the Irish with hard words, and sometimes more took place than words on both sides. The Negroes infiltrated and the Jews moved out, but with little friction, as the Jews did not tend to emphasis the color line. Long after the Negroes, came bulldozers of urban redevelopment." In reality, Mattapan was no different than any other emerging Streetcar Suburb, with ease of transportation, new housing of rapidly built two family houses and three deckers on newly laid out streets, it attracted a widely divergent segment of Bostonians. Russell says that "Jewish shops with their foreign wares and Kosher signs began to appear along Blue Hill Avenue, starting at Franklin Park, and each year creeping closer to Dorchester [Wellington] Hill. Side street after side street, district after district, became solidly Jewish… Dorchester [and Mattapan] was becoming the most thickly populated district in greater Boston."

After the fire that destroyed Chelsea, Massachusetts in 1908, many Jews began to migrate towards Roxbury, Dorchester and Mattapan. From 1880 to 1914 it was said that three million Jews had immigrated to this country from Eastern Europe. Here one could see on Blue Hill Avenue the "shops with their Kosher signs and strange wares- pumpernickel bread, rollmops, poppy-seed cakes, bagels, odd-looking fish and tripes and wrinkled sausage hanging on long skewers in the butcher shop windows." Within a decade, Mattapan had evolved into a neighborhood in its own right, though still technically a part of Dorchester. With numerous public schools for the burgeoning population of school age children, places of worship that included Episcopal, Methodist, Presbyterian, Roman Catholic churches and Jewish shuls and the opening in 1929 of the new Ashmont to Mattapan High-Speed Trolley that replaced the old railroad line of the 19th century, and which is in *Ripley's Believe It or Not* as the only trolley in the world to travel through a (Cedar Grove) cemetery, the area quickly expanded and shops and markets provided the necessities of life.

By the 1930s Mattapan had become an inclusive neighborhood with residents representing a thriving nexus of cultures, ethnicity and religion. Off the principal streets of Blue Hill

Avenue and River, Morton, Norfolk and Babson Streets new side streets were laid out and residences were built on small lots of land that spanned the gamut of one and two family houses, three deckers and apartment buildings which were built for the new residents. With ease of transportation and connections to the subway via the Mattapan to Ashmont streetcar and the streetcars along Blue Hill Avenue connecting to Egleston Square and Dudley Street, both on the Boston Elevated Railway to Boston. By the 1940s, when the streetcars that had served Mattapan since 1900 began to be replaced with trackless trolleys as the beginning of a series of changes that would come in order to accommodate the growing number of automobiles passing through the area. Places of worship in Mattapan began in the late 19th century with the Mattapan Baptist Church, the Mattapan Methodist Church, the Church of the Holy Spirit, the Berean Chapel, St. Paul's Presbyterian Church and St. Angela Merici Roman Catholic Church. There were also numerous Jewish places of worship in the 20th century that included Temple Beth Hillel, Temple Beth El, Congregation Hadrath Israel, Beth Jacob Anshe Sfard, Congregation Kehillath Jacob, Congregation Ohel Torah, Agudath Israel, Chevra Shomrei Shabbos, Shaar Tselosa Avraham, Mikvah Israel and Congregation Young Israel of Mattapan. The increase of population included almost 90,000 Jewish people living in the area from Franklin Field to Mattapan Square.

With not just public transportation but the ascendancy of the automobile the neighborhood was also a community with markets such as National D Store, A&P Market, Purity Supreme Market and small shops that catered to residents, many of them Jewish and *kosher*. Blue Hill Avenue in particular was lined with shops, stores and restaurants as well as places of entertainment such as the Morton Theatre, the Oriental Theatre and the Mattapan Theatre. Places such as Teen Town at Morton Plaza and the Chez Vous Rollerway, the G&G Delicatessen, Simco's by the Bridge, Ye Olde Brown Jug, Embers, Blue Hills Restaurant, Brothers Deli, Blackie's Deli- Haus and the Talbot Bowladrome. There was Cote Motor Company and John F. Duby selling the latest model Fords, Visnick Brothers Motors selling Studebakers, the Pontiac Dealership, John J. Delaney selling Chevrolets and Lee Motor Sales that catered to the ascendancy of the automobile. The Boston Nature Center and Wild Life Sanctuary of Mass Audubon Society, on the site of the former Mattapan State Hospital, and the Mattapan Community Health Center offer green space and healthcare. Each of these places, whether ones of worship, medical, recreational, entertainment, shopping, dining or car dealerships added to the overlay of Mattapan as a thriving neighborhood.

However, the demographics in Mattapan began to change as recounted by Francis Hamburger Russell. In the 1940s "some of the more prosperous second-generation Jews began to move away to the garden suburbs of Brookline and Newton. Much of their Torah tradition was left behind in the kahal [community.]" Throughout the United States in the 1950s, city dwellers were moving to the suburbs and the Jews of Roxbury, Dorchester, and Mattapan were no exception. However, that exodus escalated precipitously in the 1960s as unscrupulous real-estate agents employed block-busting tactics, street violence grew, and, starting in 1968, the consortium known as the Boston Banks Urban Renewal Group (B-BURG) attempted to reverse decades of discrimination by providing accessible mortgages to African American homebuyers in targeted areas, including streets in and around Dorchester and Mattapan.

Mattapan changed in the late 1960s and 1970s but it also began to embrace a new middle class, as in the late 20th century Haitians, Bahamians, Jamaicans and others from Caribbean countries began to purchase homes in Mattapan and like the new residents of a century before, agreed that the location and the ease of transportation were major reasons to invest in the neighborhood by purchasing houses. Mattapan, said to be the largest Haitian community in Massachusetts, is today an inclusive neighborhood of people of all walks of life, all races, ethnicity and religions and embraces many first- generation immigrants. It is truly the melting pot of Boston with Blue Hill Avenue as its main artery.

"I Like Ike" and it sure looked like the residents of Mattapan and Dorchester also liked him as well! Dwight D. Eisenhower is seen in 1952 waving to the crowd from a black Cadillac Series 62 convertible, with Mamie Doud Eisenhower seated beside him, during his campaign for the presidency of the United States. On the left is a campaign sign for Jeanne Brody Weisberg, president of the New England Branch of the National Women's League of the United Synagogues of America, who was running for the Massachusetts Senate. The crowd is seen along Blue Hill Avenue with shops that include C. Hoffman's Children's and Ladies Wear, Murray's Shoes, Blue Hill Meat Market, Glickman's Hardware, Sam & Harold's Fruit Market, Moller's Bakery, Cohen Shoes and just out of view Waldman's Candies.

1

EARLY MATTAPAN

The Hobart House was one of the few houses built in the early 19th century in the part of Dorchester that was to become known as Mattapan. Norfolk Avenue, which connected Codman Square and Mattapan Square, was an old Native American path much like River Street which paralleled the Neponset River and which eventually connected to Dedham, but these houses were often set on large farms near the road. The area was called *Unquetyquissett* by the Neponset tribe of the Massachusett Indians and had early mills along the Neponset River, which had been dammed as early as 1634 to afford water power, and extensive farms along Norfolk, River, Walk Hill and Oakland (now Cummins Highway) Streets.

Looking north, Blue Hill Avenue began as the Brush Hill Turnpike. It was chartered in 1805 and although the Town of Milton disapproved, the turnpike was completed in 1809. In 1810 an act was passed applying to this road, providing that the corporation should not collect toll from anyone on military duty, on religious duty, coming to or from any grist mill, or on the common or ordinary business of family concerns, or from anyone who had not been out of town with a loaded team or carriage. Seen in 1870 on the right, at the then corner of Norfolk Street, is the James Boies House, he being a partner of John McLean in the Boies and McLean Paper Mill at Unquetyquissett, later referred to as Mattapan, and who led the teamsters, hostlers, farriers and ox-drivers to Dorchester Heights in 1776 that resulted in the Evacuation of Boston by the British and Loyalists. Blue Hill Avenue was widened beginning in 1894 and the right side was demolished.

Brush Hill Turnpike was laid out in 1805 as a turnpike road connecting Roxbury with towns to the south, and one paid a toll at toll houses along the turnpike road according to the weight of the cart load, which was often hay being sent to Boston. The toll house at the corner of River Street is seen on the left; unfortunately the toll road never brought in sufficient revenues and failed in 1856 when the Brush Hill Turnpike Corporation relinquished its franchise. In this circa 1870 photograph, Blue Hill Avenue, as it was renamed in 1870 looking north, remained a rural and largely agrarian part of Dorchester well into the 19th century but after the extension of the Dorchester and Milton Branch of the Old Colony Railroad, the area began to see the beginnings of development.

The Fowler-Clark-Epstein Farm has an historic house that was built in the 1786 by Samuel Fowler, and which included a 300 acre farm between what is today Morton Street and Blue Hill Avenue. The land was sold to the Clark family in the early 19th century and after Dorchester was annexed to the city of Boston in 1870 would later be subdivided into building lots on new streets laid out through the former farm. Woolson, Hosmer, Clarkwood and Evelyn Streets were laid out in the 1890s connecting Norfolk Street and Blue Hill Avenue, but the colonial farmhouse remained intact on a small lot and was purchased in 1941 by Jorge Epstein, a jeweler with Firestone and Parson and later an architectural salvage dealer at Old Mansions in Mattapan. Epstein embellished the house with wall murals and used reclaimed and salvaged architectural details from Boston buildings to embellish the grounds. Today, after being restored through Historic Boston, this is the Urban Farming Institute.

The Stern House was typical of the small houses built in Mattapan in the 19th century. Family members, including the family horses, pose in front of the home of Edward and Sarah Holmes Stern at 2 Fremont Street, at the corner of Blue Hill Avenue, in the late 19th century. Beginning in the late 1880s, the new houses built on the side streets off Blue Hill Avenue were springing up, as if by magic and would continue unabated for the next few decades. Whether built as a family home or for speculative purposes, the neighborhood embraced the change with a variety of housing options. In 1955 the house was replaced with the Alfred D. Thomas Funeral Home, which is now Barron Chiropractic & Rehabilitation. (Courtesy Joan Stern)

Senator John Conness, seen on the far right in a bowler hat, is haying the field in front of his house on River Street in the 1880s. Conness was a senator from California whose support of the federal land grants for Yosemite Valley and Mariposa Grove, founded what later became the Yosemite National Park; he also supported immigration and civil rights for Chinese immigrants in California which were two of his enduring legacies. In retirement he moved to Boston and purchased a large estate between Dorchester Lower Mills and Mattapan Square. Seen in the 1880s family and friends hay the field which was a common chore during the late 19th century, and fill the horse-drawn hay wagon on the left, which slowly became less commonplace as farms and estates were subdivided for development. Today the Conness House is part of the Boston Medical Center.

The Liversidge Institute was founded in 1881 through a generous bequest of Thomas Liversidge. Stephen Liversidge, and later his son Thomas, was a manufacturer of starch with a factory on the Neponset River. In 1852 they were awarded a diploma for excellence of their product from the Maryland Institute Fair. The starch factory was immensely successful and allowed Thomas Liversidge to endow the Institute with $300,000 whose proceeds were "intended to afford a home and good literary and industrial education to orphans and other destitute boys who must be natives of either New England or Old England." The massive building with a center tower and a three-sided piazza survived until 1943 when it was destroyed by fire. Today the estate has numerous houses and Ridgeview Avenue follows the original driveway.

The large shed-like Mattapan Depot of the Dorchester and Milton Branch of the Old Colony Railroad was built in 1872 with an adjoining freight house as the terminus of the line, having branched off the Central Division and continuing with stations at Neponset, Granite Bridge (the junction with the Shawmut Branch OCRR) in Dorchester and Milton Village and Central Avenue in Milton, and the terminus at Mattapan. The line began in 1847, with two round-trips to Boston daily, and was leased to the Old Colony Railroad from 1848 to 1856, and operated under contract by the Old Colony from 1856 to 1863, when it was merged into the Old Colony and Fall River Railroad Company. In 1893, it became part of the New York, New Haven and Hartford Railroad as part of the lease of the entire Old Colony Railroad network. This wood-framed depot with its bold sign with gilt letters was replaced by a Roxbury pudding stone ticket office and waiting room which still stands. On the far left was a corner of the James Boies House.

The J.H. Burt & Company factory was on Blue Hill Avenue at Fairway Street in Mattapan Square. The company was founded in 1850 by John Holland Burt and his brother George Lathe Burt and did a tremendous contracting business, providing milled lumber for the new houses and stores being built in Mattapan, Dorchester, Milton and Quincy in the late 19th century. In fact, the Burt Brothers also built speculative housing on Oakland Street (now Cummins Highway) as well as many houses by commission in Mattapan, Dorchester and Milton. Seen in 1895, employees of Burt Brothers pose in front of the factory with their horse-drawn delivery wagons.

The junction of River Street, seen straight ahead, Oakland Street (now Cummins Highway) and Blue Hill Avenue had been built up by the late 19th century, with a horse trough in the center. In the distance on the left is the Hersey House and barn and on the right the Fleming House. On the far right is the Bartlett Block with the Mattapan Post Office on the left and Charles Wentworth's Pharmacy on the ground floor, and just to the left center is Oakland Hall with its pyramidal style caps on the four corners of the building, which was the location of the Mattapan Reading Room, a performance hall and where many groups including the Knights of Columbus, the Catholic Daughters and Eastern Star met. Built in 1872 by Amor Hollingsworth, owner of the Tileston and Hollingsworth Paper Company, he left a library trust fund that eventually benefited the Boston Public Library branch in Mattapan. In 1929 Oakland Street was renamed in honor of Reverend John F. Cummins, pastor of the Sacred Heart Church in Roslindale.

The Bartlett Block was a large two-story commercial block built in 1890 by J.H. Burt & Company for Jonathan B.L. Bartlett, who moved to Mattapan in 1873 and built his house at 459 River Street. He began his career as a letter carrier and later became manager of the Mattapan Post Office where it was said that he "conducted it so well that it was officially pronounced the best conducted office of its kind in the country." Bartlett made a major career change in 1894 and became involved in real estate, serving as treasurer and manager of the Blue Hill Terrace Company, which developed land in Mattapan, as well as in Milton in the areas around Hudson Street, Blue Hill Terrace Street and Thacher Street. He also served as a congressman in the Massachusetts House of Representatives from Ward 24, Mattapan. Seen about 1910, the Mattapan Post Office and Wentworth's Mattapan Pharmacy, whose "soda fountain is a cherished memory" of Maureen Ferris, are on the ground floor of the Bartlett Block; the block was demolished in the early 1950s. The statue *Rise* by Karen Eutemeny today marks the entrance of Blue Hill Avenue into Mattapan as a gateway to Boston.

Looking north on Blue Hill Avenue, the Bartlett Block, the Obert Block and the J.H. Burt & Company Mill can be seen on the western side of the avenue. In the Bartlett Block was the Mattapan Post Office, Charles Wentworth's Mattapan Pharmacy, with its gilded mortar-and-pestle signboard, the Mattapan Laundry, the Mattapan Creamery, Burkhart Brothers and various offices including a dentist on the second floor. Notice the three-story building on the right, wedged between Blue Hill Avenue on the left and Norfolk Street on the right, advertising soda and cigars on either side of the center door. The right side would be demolished in 1894 when Blue Hill Avenue was widened between River and Babcock Streets in the early 1920s.

By the early 20th century Mattapan Square had been built up with the Burt Block, built by the Burt Brothers in 1893 seen with its distinctive wood tower and dormered roof, on the left and the new stone depot of the New York, New Haven and Hartford Railroad. Electric streetcars can be seen on Blue Hill Avenue on the left and emerging from River Street in the center. With the widening of Blue Hill Avenue in 1894, the neighborhood was served by the Boston Elevated streetcar, the Old Colony Street Railway and the Blue Hill Street Railway all of which used Mattapan Station. Notice the wood electric utility poles with glass insulators on the left, extending along the length of Blue Hill Avenue.

The junction of River Street, on the right, and Blue Hill Avenue in the late 1920s shows the Burt Block still a prominent anchor on the corner of River Street with numerous businesses including the Frank Cantor Tailoring Shop and the Joseph Horak Furrier and Designer Shop. The new shops on the left including the Lanata Block, with its twin pedimented roof cornice, which was designed by A.D. Boyle and built in 1920 for Joseph Lanata. In the distance can be seen the spire of St. Angela Church, now Our Lady of Mount Carmel Parish. The tracks seen in the foreground are being reconfigured to serve the new Mattapan Station which would open in 1929 and connect it to Ashmont Station via a high-speed orange PCC streetcar. Interestingly, this streetcar is listed in *Ripley's Believe It or Not* as the only streetcar in the world to have access through a cemetery, the Cedar Grove Cemetery. The statue *Rise* by Fern Cunningham marks the entrance of Blue Hill Avenue into Mattapan as a gateway to Boston. (Courtesy of Frank Cheney)

PLACES OF WORSHIP

This is the elegant interior of Agudath Israel Anshei Sfard at 220 Woodrow Avenue in Dorchester. Agudath Israel of America is an American organization that represents Haredi Orthodox Jews, and is loosely affiliated with the International World Agudath Israel. Agudah seeks to meet the needs of the Haredi community, advocates for its religious and civil rights, and services its constituents through charitable, educational, and social service projects across North America. The Torahs of Agudath Israel were stored in a magnificent wood ark and bimah with gilded capitals on the pilasters, a pair of lions rampant on either side of two tablets of the Ten Commandments and surmounted by a gilded eagle, that enshrines the sacred Torah scrolls that were used for worship. Notice the electric light bulb menorah and the pews with the Star of David in a carved circle on the sides. (Courtesy of Sandler Family Archives)

The Church of the Holy Spirit was founded in 1886 at Mattapan Square and was designed by Arthur Rotch and Thomas Tilden and built at the corner of River and Oakland Streets (now Cummins Highway.) The church was given by Annie Rotch Lamb in memory of her father Benjamin Smith Rotch, as well as the Parish House which she gave in memory of her mother Annie Bigelow Rotch. The architectural firm of Rotch and Tilden was organized by partners Arthur Rotch and George Tilden, both of whom were graduated from the Massachusetts Institute of Technology School of Architecture and L'École des Beaux-Arts in Paris. Keith Morgan said of the church that "The massive shingled tower, with rows of great louvered vents that impart an oriental flavor to the design, dominates the Latin cross plan, constructed of local pudding stone with half-timbering in the gable ends." Ralph Adams Cram later designed the Parish House in 1909. (Author's Collection)

The Mattapan Methodist Church, originally built as an Episcopal chapel, was on Norfolk (now Babson) Street and was one of the earliest churches in Mattapan, having begun as early as 1845 offering prayer meetings at the home of George Black to a small group of non-denominational worshipers. The church was a simple Queen Anne wood-framed church with a modified Palladian stained glass window on the facade, that was used by Methodists who are a "group of historically related denominations of Protestant Christianity which derive their doctrine of practice and belief from the life and teachings of John Wesley." Here they worshiped until 1924 when they voted to move to Milton and purchased land for a church and community house on the Blue Hills Parkway, and renaming it the Parkway Methodist Community Church. In 1942 the site became the Mattapan Post No. 128 American Legion, designed by Herman Freer, and today 107 Babson Street, a private residence, is on the site. (Author's collection)

St. Paul Presbyterian Church was designed by C.A. Russell and F.N. Russell, an architectural partnership of Cornelius A. Russell and Fred Newton Russell which was formed in 1903. Built in 1920 at the corner of Oakland Street (now Cummins Highway) and Rexford Street near Mattapan Square, the church was a stucco Gothic Revival design church, with two crenelated towers and two side gables with lancet stained glass windows flanking the corner tower with its cantilevered entrance porch. Presbyterianism is a part of the Reformed tradition within Protestantism, which traces its origins to Scotland. Presbyterian churches derive their name from the Presbyterian form of church government, which is governed by representative assemblies of elders. Today this is St. Paul Victory Church Assembly of God.

Established in 1907 from portions of the parishes of St. Gregory the Great in Dorchester and Most Precious Blood in Hyde Park, the lower church of St. Angela Merici Church was designed by Thomas F. Houghton, successor to Patrick J. Keeley, and completed in 1909. The upper church was designed by Maginnis and Walsh as a Romanesque Revival red brick and limestone church with an asymmetrical bell tower and was dedicated by William Cardinal O'Connell in 1919. The church was named for St. Angela Merici who has the double distinction of founding the first teaching congregation of women in the Roman Catholic Church and what is now called a "secular institute" of religious women. Today, the church is known as Our Lady of Mount Carmel Parish, an inclusive church and the spiritual home for a diverse community of Roman Catholics largely African American, Caribbean American and Haitian American united in one faith and one God while proclaiming the Gospel of Jesus-Christ. There are three masses on Sunday, with Mass said in French, English and Creole. (Author's collection)

The Berean Chapel, a branch of the Dorchester Temple Baptist Church in Codman Square in Dorchester, was built in 1900 in Mattapan and was the outgrowth of a Bible school established by the Dorchester Temple Church, assisted by the Massachusetts Baptist Sunday School Association. Located on Lauriat Avenue (now Woodrow Avenue) between Ashton and Lucerne Streets, it was a Shingle-style church with an asymmetrical crenelated tower and a large stained glass window which was the gift of the Tremont Temple Bible School in Boston. The chapel later became Congregation Hadrath Israel, which was founded in 1911 as Hadrath Kodesh in Roxbury and which moved in 1928 from 1000 Blue Hill Avenue to this building. The church was remodeled as a Synagogue by William L. Minor in 1928 with crenelated towers. In 1970 the temple merged with Temple Adas Israel in Hyde Park to become known as Adas Hadrath. Today this is the Faithful Church of Christ. (Courtesy of the Wyner Family Jewish Heritage Center at the New England Historic Genealogical Society)

Agudath Israel Anshei Sfard, founded in 1915, was designed by S.S. Eisenberg and was built in 1921 at 220 Woodrow Avenue at the corner of Lucerne Street. The impressive Classical Revival brick and stone temple has three monumental arches on the facade with lions flanking the Torah at the parapet. Samuel Saul Eisenberg of S.S. Eisenberg Associates, which was founded in 1921, designed numerous apartment buildings along Blue Hill Avenue in Dorchester and Mattapan as well as Boston's Fenway. Eisenberg, also worked closely with his partner Herman L. Feer, who was the architect of the Oriental Theatre in Mattapan Square. After the temple had a fire in 1970, it was sold in 1972 to the Temple Salem Seventh Day Adventist Church. (Courtesy of Sandler Family Archives)

Kehillath Jacob was founded in 1922 and was originally on Ormond Street when it relocated to 18 Fessenden Street. The original shul, seen on the right, was designed by Saul Elias Moffie who was a graduate of the Tufts University School of Engineering. It was built in 1927 of red brick and cement and had two entrances with the Ten Commandments directly above. In 1954 Arthur Winebaum AIA, a graduate of the Massachusetts Institute of Technology, designed a new community social hall, with classrooms in the basement, which was built to the left. The temple was sold 1972 to the State Temple Church of God in Christ. (Courtesy of the Wyner Family Jewish Heritage Center at the New England Historic Genealogical Society)

Yeshiva Ohel Torah Congregation was founded in 1948 and was located in a former one-family house at 149 Greenfield (originally Randolph) Road, at the corner of Rugby Road, with remodeling for worship done by Saverio Pizzario for the shul. The building was sold in 1980 when the congregation left Mattapan and today it is a private residence. (Courtesy of the Wyner Family Jewish Heritage Center at the New England Historic Genealogical Society)

Temple Beth Hillel was designed by Eisenberg and Feer, an architectural partnership of Samuel S. Eisenberg and Herman L. Feer, and built in 1921 at 800 Morton Street near Norfolk Street. Built of brick with limestone details, it was a Classical Revival synagogue with the Ten Commandments at the roof parapet. Along with the Dorchester and Mattapan Hebrew School, which was built to the left, and the Dorchester Manor, a banqueting room and entertainment center in the lower hall, it was a thriving center for worship, education and socializing. In 1970, Temple Beth Hillel left its historic building in Mattapan and merged with Beth Torah in West Roxbury to become Temple Hillel B'nai Torah. Today, this is Berea Seventh Day Adventist Church and School.

Young Israel of Mattapan was chartered in 1934 and was located at 1099 Blue Hill Avenue near Johnston Road. Originally a two-family house owned by Jennie Weisman, it was remodeled in 1939 by Saul Elias Moffie, a graduate of the Tufts University School of Engineering and a well- known architect, with a new brick facade and square porch piers and a rear room for religious purposes. The building was sold 1970 and the congregation merged with Young Israel in Randolph, along with Congregation Kehilath Jacob. This is now St. Luke Christian African Methodist Episcopal Zion Church. (Courtesy of the Wyner Family Jewish Heritage Center at the New England Historic Genealogical Society)

The Morning Star Baptist Church was designed by Stull and Lee Architects and built in 2002 at 1257 Blue Hill Avenue. Originally the site of the Schlossberg Funeral Home which opened in 1953, the lot has steep rock cliffs that had to be blasted for a level building lot. The church was founded in 1965 and relocated to this spot in 1976. In 1981, Bishop John M. Borders, III became pastor and under his leadership that the church has experienced its most significant growth. Rev. Borders and his associate ministers have been highly successful in bridging generations, attracting younger church members while continuing to fulfill the needs of more senior members. "Morning Star Baptist Church is committed to improving the quality of spiritual and economic life for its membership and for residents of the surrounding community." Along Blue Hill Avenue today are the Greater Victory Temple, Lily of the Valley Baptist Church, Jubilee Church, Blue Hill Missionary Baptist Church, New Jerusalem Church of God and Eglise Methodiste Libre Hatienne de Boston.

3

PLACES OF EDUCATION

The Dorchester Mattapan Hebrew School was designed by Samuel Saul Eisenberg and Herman L. Feer, and built in 1921 at 800 Morton Street near Norfolk Street. Supplemental Hebrew schools had been established in the early 20th Century to educate children attending public schools about Jewish history, culture, and rituals with a focus on Hebrew literacy. The Dorchester Mattapan Hebrew School was intensive, meeting five days a week, unlike many of its suburban counterparts which met just three. On the Sabbath, students could employ their newfound skills at children's services. Most students ended their formal Jewish education when they became "bnai mitzvah," the age of adulthood at 12 or 13, but advanced classes were offered for those who had greater interest. Seen here in 1957, the graduates of the Dorchester Mattapan Hebrew School pose for their class photograph with their Rabbis, educators and staff.

The Solomon Lewenberg Junior High School was designed by Desmond and Lord and built in 1930 on Outlook Road, the crest of Wellington Hill. An impressive Classical Revival design of red brick and limestone, it has an impressive entrance with four monumental Ionic columns supporting an entablature and flanking wings. Solomon Lewenberg, for whom the school was named, was a public-spirited man and well known for his philanthropy. He was especially interested in welfare projects in the Dorchester and Mattapan neighborhoods, and was appointed to the Gas and Electric Light Commission by Governor Samuel McCall. Mr. Lewenberg was a member of the board of trustees of Temple Ohabei Shalom in Brookline. The school closed in 2010 and is now the Young Achievers Science and Mathematics Pilot School.

The Roger Wolcott School was designed by Everett and Mead, an architectural partnership of Arthur G. Everett and Samuel W. Mead, and built of red brick and limestone in 1901 at the corner of Norfolk and Morton Streets; on the left is a three decker at 447 Norfolk Street designed by S.S. Eisenberg and built in 1922 for Israel and Sarah Conviser. The school was named for Roger Wolcott, who served as lieutenant governor of Massachusetts from 1893 to 1897, becoming Acting Governor in 1896 upon the death of Governor Frederic T. Greenhalge. He was elected governor in his own right in 1897 and served until 1900. The school was destroyed by fire, and was demolished in 1980. Today, it is the site of a Walgreen's store.

The Pauline Agassiz Shaw School was designed by James E. McLaughlin and built in 1919 at the corner of Norfolk Avenue and Morton Street. A Classical Revival brick and concrete school, it had cement urns at the roof over the entrances and swag lintels. Mrs. Shaw was a pioneer in the kindergarten movement, personally funding dozens of programs throughout the city, in addition to supporting the North Bennet Street School in the North End. Her husband, Quincy Adams Shaw, was said to be the wealthiest man in New England upon his death in 1917 and they donated numerous works of art including the *Madonna in the Clouds*, the first piece of Renaissance sculpture to be donated to the Museum of Fine Arts.

The Martha A. Baker School was designed by the Department of School Buildings and built in 1931 at 630 Walk Hill Street. Martha Alberta Baker was the daughter of Captain Lorenzo Dow Baker who in 1870 created the modern banana production industry. In 1881 he partnered with Elisha Hopkins to form L.D. Baker & Co. and later with Andrew W. Preston and eight others founded the Boston Fruit Company, which led to several successive partnerships, ending in the 1899 formation of the United Fruit Company, now Chiquita Brands International. Martha Baker was graduated from Lasalle College for Women and lived in Boston, Jamaica and at *Belvernon*, her estate in Wellfleet on Cape Cod. She was an heir of United Fruit Company and became a noted philanthropist like her father. A member of the Universal Peace Congress and the Society of Mayflower Descendants, she took an active interest in education and the less fortunate often educating Jamaicans at Tilton Academy and the school was named in her honor.

The William Bradford School was designed by the Department of School Buildings and built in 1918 at 55 Willowwood Street. The school was named for the second governor of Plymouth Bay Colony Bradford was not only a leader of the Pilgrims having arrived on the *Mayflower* in 1620, but also the author of the journal *Of Plimoth Plantation,* in which he drew deep parallels between everyday life and events in the Bible. This journal was kept from 1620 to 1646, and Bradford is considered by historians to be "one of the most influential of the Pilgrim settlers for his outstanding leadership, his desire to steadfastly hold to his religious and moral ideals and his determination to keep Plymouth a thriving and independent colony." He has been called "The Father of American History" as his journal is not simply a recounting of the history of the Pilgrims from their emigration from England to the New World, but truly the story of the founding of America. Today the site is townhouses.

The Charles Logue School was designed by Mulhall & Holmes Architects and Engineers and built in 1923 on Walk Hill Street, adjacent to the Martha A. Baker School. The school was named for Charles Logue, an Irish immigrant, who founded the Charles Logue Building Company. According to Boston Irish historian Dennis Ryan, Charles Logue became a major contractor in Boston, building the Boston College campus as well as churches and schools for the city's Archdiocese. He also constructed Fenway Park, the home of the Boston Red Sox. Ground was broken for the park in September 1911. The official opening took place on April 20, 1912. Cardinal William O'Connell hailed Charles as a "man beloved by everybody who knew him." Today it is apartments.

The James J. Chittick School was designed by M.A. Dyer Company Architects and built in 1931 at 154 Ruskindale Road. Michael Andrew Dyer was graduated from the Massachusetts Institute of Technology and founded his own firm in 1924, specializing in the design of public buildings and hospitals. The Right Reverend Monsignor James J. Chittick, for whom the school was named, was the second pastor of the Church of the Most Precious Blood in Hyde Park. Beloved by Christian and Jew alike, he was said to be an able administrator, builder, educator, pastor, and a true alter Christus.

The Charles H. Taylor School was designed by the Department of School Buildings and built in 1931 at 1060 Morton Street at Pineridge Street. Taylor was the manager and editor of the *Boston Globe*, founded in 1872 by six Boston businessmen led by Eben Dyer Jordan, beginning in 1873. Having begun his career as a reporter for the *Boston Traveler*, and later serving as private secretary to Governor William Claflin, he would create a newspaper that "laid down a strict rule that all news should be given impartially." *The Boston Globe* would evolve into the most important newspaper in New England, under the leadership of four generations of the Taylor family.

The Audubon School was designed by James E. McLaughlin and built in 1918 at 436 Harvard Street. The school was named for John James Audubon who was an American ornithologist, naturalist, and skillful and detailed painter. His combined interests in art and ornithology turned into a plan to make a complete pictorial record of all the bird species of North America. The former school was repurposed in 1990 as the Audubon Apartments which is near the Massachusetts Audubon Nature Preserve, and which was built on part of the site that formerly housed both the Shattuck and Audubon Hospitals.

Temple Beth Hillel, seen on the right, had the Dorchester and Mattapan Hebrew School adjacent to it on the left. The school was designed by Eisenberg and Feer, an architectural partnership of Samuel S. Eisenberg and Herman L. Feer, and built in 1921 at 800 Morton Street near Norfolk Street. As a Talmud Torah school, it was considered a supplementary school whose students attended public schools during the day. There were also other Hebrew schools, the Hashachar Hebrew School at 1006 Blue Hill Avenue and the Mattapan Religious School on Woodrow Avenue, where it was thought, and hoped, that these schools would create "an educated American Jew who would have access in the original language to the sources of Jewish tradition."

St. Angela School was the grammar school of St. Angela Merici Parish in Mattapan and was designed by Richard J. Shaw and built in 1935. Shaw was a prominent architect in Boston who specialized in ecclesiastical design and was architect of the Hatch Shell on Boston's Esplanade. Located at 120 Babson Street, the school was named for St. Angela who founded the Company of St. Ursula in 1535 in Brescia, in which women dedicated their lives to the service of the Church through the education of girls. From this organization evolved the Order of Ursulines, whose nuns established places of prayer and learning. This later became the Saint John Paul II Catholic Academy which closed in 2018. Today, the Mattahunt School and the Ellison Parks Early Education School (formerly the Mattapan Early Education Center) continue to educate the youth of 21st century Mattapan.

4

MATTAPAN SQUARE

Streetcar 5621 turns into Mattapan Station from Blue Hill Avenue in 1945 seen with a spider web of overhead wires. Mattapan Square by the mid-20th century had become a thriving commercial district with shops, stores, restaurants and offices that offered everything under the sun. In the center is the Obert Block, a wood-frame and dormered commercial block built by Burt Brothers in the 1890s with shops on the ground floor and offices above and the Lanata Block to the right, which was designed by A.D. Boyle and built in 1920 for Joseph Lanata. The stores on the far left were designed by Eisenberg and Feer and built in 1931 to replace the Bartlett Block. The blue enamel facade building is the Blue Hills Cafeteria and Cocktail Lounge with its tall neon sign.

The elm tree shaded depot of the New York, New Haven and Hartford Railroad, later known as the Mattapan Station, seen in 1910, was originally the depot of the Dorchester and Milton Branch of the Old Colony Railroad, later the station of the Ashmont to Mattapan High Speed trolley. Built of Roxbury pudding stone in 1901 with a gable of rough cast cement and wood in a Tudoresque style, it had a prominent clock set in a rondel; commuters could purchase tickets to Boston, with a covered waiting area on the right. To the left of the depot was a granite horse trough donated in 1905 by Horatio and Annie Lawrence Lamb. Today this is Kuizinn Lakay Plus after many years as Papa Gino's Pizza. On the left is a Boston El car on River Street going to Forest Hills Station from the Lower Mills. (Courtesy of Frank Cheney)

The Mattapan Theatre, once known as the Anderson Theatre and fondly as the Little Matty, was opened in 1910 and was subsequently known as the Scenic Temple Theatre until 1926 when it was renamed the Mattapan Theatre; set on its roof above the entrance was a huge Art Deco neon sign which advertised the movies du jour. The theater was showing *This Thing They Called Love* and *Nobody's Children*. Later used as the temporary Mattapan Post Office, today this is Hair Stop. The theater was wedged between the Mattapan Wine Liquor Store (originally the Blue Willow Restaurant,) which advertised Croft Ale which was brewed in Jamaica Plain from 1934 to 1952 on the left, the Mattapan Depot, which was converted to commercial purposes in 1929 and later as Cathay Village. On the far right can be seen the awning of the Atlas Diner, designed by the J.G. Brill Company as the "Universal," a small all-steel diner. At one time there was a Civil War cannon and a triangular stack of cannonballs here that was dedicated "In Memory of Our Soldiers" by the Mattapan Improvement Association; the base of this monument, devoid of its cannon, is now in front of the William E. Carter American Legion Post No. 16 in Mattapan Square.

Streetcar No. 4285 turns from Cummins Highway at River Street onto Blue Hill Avenue in 1930 at Mattapan Square and is headed to Campello via the Eastern Massachusetts Street Railway Company. Campello was a neighborhood of Brockton where there were numerous manufacturing establishments of boots, shoes, cabinet furniture, and musical instruments. The streetcar from Mattapan offered workers accessibility to numerous jobs. The Bartlett Block, which was at the corner of Cummins Highway and Blue Hill Avenue, is seen in the center, and on the far right is the spire of St. Angela Merici Roman Catholic (now Our Lady of Mount Carmel) Church on Blue Hill Avenue at Fremont Street. The statues by Fern Cuningham and Karen Eutemeny known as *Rise* mark the entrance to Mattapan. (Courtesy of Frank Cheney)

Looking north on Blue Hill Avenue, two-story commercial blocks were built in the 1920s; on the left is the Lanata Block that had the First National Store, and the Fairway Building with Brigham's, Borden's Barber Shop, the Colonial Bookstore, Morosini Fruit Store and Dine's Hardware. On the right were one-story commercial blocks that included a multitude of stores that included W.T. Grant, Woolworth's, Bob and Oscar's Deli, Murray's Department Store and many other shops and stores with a parking lot in the rear for shoppers. In the center can be seen the tall neon sign of the Oriental Theatre, which was brilliant with colored neon lights in the evening. There was also Ember's Restaurant owned by Happy Sidell which one person recalled had "Rotisserie chickens cooking and spinning in the window....they smelled so good so I made my Grandfather take me in." In the distance is the spire of St. Angela Merici Roman Catholic Church on the right and the Midland Division Bridge in the distance, which had the overhead bridge removed in 1944. (Courtesy of Frank Cheney)

Streetcar 5133, headed towards Mattapan Station, passes the Oriental Theatre, with its Chinese-inspired facade with red terra cotta tile roofs inspired by the Street Gate of Tsinanfu. The marquee, with Chinese detailing and miniature oriental roofs, advertises in 1938 *Adventures of Tom Sawyer*, a drama with Tommy Kelly, Jackie Moran and May Robson, and *Everybody Sing*, a musical comedy starring Allan Jones, Judy Garland and Fanny Brice. The theater, with its magical blue sky with moving clouds and twinkling lights emulating stars, had oriental figures set in niches along the walls, the eyes of which were illuminated in red when the house lights went down. There was also a Wurlitzer organ, Opus 2131, which was installed along the side of the second floor of the theater in 1930 which added greatly to the entertainment. On the left is the Mattapan Supply Company and the Mattapan Post Office, and just out of view the Hobby Fair Store. Today this is the Frugal Furniture Outlet Store. (Courtesy of Frank Cheney)

In 1929 a Boston El Type Four streetcar between Ashmont and Mattapan had replaced the Dorchester and Milton Branch of the Old Colony Railroad. Seen in the center is an early streetcar in the barbed wire fenced River Street trailer yard. On the right are, as Daniel White says "seven hole-in-the-wall businesses" built adjacent to the former Mattapan Depot. It was in one of these shops that Cathay Village was located. The Chinese restaurant was opened in 1953 by King Sam Yung and later owned by Andrew Chin; one former patron said "I just LOVED however they did their brown sauces, like over the egg foo young and beef with broccoli. My mother was enamored of Chinese food and asked for the food by the Chinese name, she was very proud that she knew that "gai" was chicken…Loved ordering "char shel dang" (I don't recall what that was, maybe a pork and vegetables dish? I'm not sure) and moo goo gai pan." Unfortunately Cathay Village was closed 1984.

Mattapan Station was built in the late 1920s as the terminus of the Ashmont-to-Mattapan High Speed trolley line. These two streetcars, No. 6244 on the left and No. 5730, emerge from the newly built cement reinforced station with the parapet boldly proclaiming "Mattapan." By the 1930s, this was a major connector not just to Ashmont Station, but streetcars from Roxbury, Roslindale, Hyde Park, Milton as well as points to the south. The Fairmount Line of the MBTA Commuter Rail also serves Mattapan at the Morton Street and Blue Hill Avenue stations, providing service to downtown Boston and the suburbs. Today, the Dallas cars with their distinctive style service the Ashmont to Mattapan line. (Courtesy of Frank Cheney)

The one-story cast stone and brick commercial block along Blue Hill Avenue was designed by H.E. Richards and built in 1923 and there was a variety of shops that ranged from an auto dealership, barber shops, beauty salons and specialty shops. Among the many businesses in the mid-20th century were John J. Delaney Chevrolet, Alson's Men's Shop, Reliable Hardware Company, Karen's Buttercup Donut Shop, Ember's Restaurant, Belle's Bakery, Brigham's, Klein's Shoe Store, Carroll's Cut Rate, Mailly Jewelers, Woolworth's, Kennedy's Butter and Eggs, Gaffin Shoes, W.T. Grant's, Blackie's Deli, Murray's Department Store. In the back adjacent to the parking lot was Walsh Sporting Goods Store.

Looking south along Blue Hill Avenue towards River Street, the Shawmut Bank, with its Indian logo on the sign board, is on one side of Fairway Street, and the other side is the Fairway Building built in 1930 by Amor and Valentine Hollingsworth with Brigham's, along with Dainty Dot Dresses, and the Dorothy Muriel Bakery. Just around the corner on River Street behind Blanchard's Liquors was Santospirito's Market whose cheerful motto was "Bring your dough to Manny and Joe, they'll make the bread." Notice Great Blue Hill in the distance, the name given by the Puritans who, while sailing along the coastline, noticed the bluish hue of the exposed granite faces when viewed from a distance, which was due to riebeckite. Not only was the hill to give its name to Blue Hill Avenue (and previously the turnpike) but also to WGBH, the public radio station founded in 1951 using Great Blue Hill which is the original location in Milton, Massachusetts of the transmitter.

Blue Hill Avenue by the late 1950s had a median strip in the center with dual street lights replacing the overhead wires for the streetcars as buses now provided transportation. Notice Woolworth on the left with a large billboard on the roof advertising Pabst Beer which obviously "Makes it Perfect." Pabst Blue Ribbon, commonly abbreviated PBR, is an American lager beer that has been brewed since 1844 by Pabst Brewing Company. On the right is the Oriental Theatre, which has had its vertical neon sign removed and its marquee remodeled in 1956 when the sidewalk was cutback to widen the avenue. The dense row of trees seen in the distance is along the Neponset River on the Milton side of the granite bridge.

Looking north on Blue Hill Avenue from River Street, pedestrians cross towards Mattapan Station in the late 1970s. Notice the profusion of billboards as one enters the square from Milton as well as how heavy both automobile and delivery truck traffic was during the business day. On the left is Mark Greeting Cards, Jimmy's Diner, Bell's Bakery and the Tom English Tap. By the 1960s, Thomas English had opened numerous bars that he and later his family owned and operated throughout the city of Boston including the neighborhoods of Dorchester, West Roxbury, Hyde Park, Mattapan, Mission Hill, South Boston, Quincy and Cambridge.

River Street, looking east from Blue Hill Avenue, was one of the oldest streets in Mattapan having originally been an Indian trail and laid out in the 17th century by the Puritans paralleling the Neponset River and connected Dorchester to Dedham. On the left is a one-story commercial block that replaced the Burt Block and Celi's "The Man's Hair Stylist." On the right is the Terminal Barber Shop in the former Atlas Diner, and Papa Gino's, a pizza chain founded in 1961 by Michael Valerio. Originally known as Piece O' Pizza in East Boston the store had an immensely popular pizza parlor in the former Mattapan Depot.

Looking north on Blue Hill Avenue from River Street towards Babson Street, the bustling one-story commercial block had numerous shops, including from the right Ann's Corset Shop, Royal Cleaners, Dainty Dress, Brother's Deli and Restaurant, Klein's Shoe Store, Cummings, First National Bank, W.T. Grant Company, Woolworth's and many more. Notice the large number of taxi cabs, conveniently double parked, on Blue Hill Avenue awaiting their next fare.

Passengers board an MBTA bus that just departed Mattapan Station and is headed to Roxbury's Egleston Square Station, a station on the Boston Elevated Railway Line, later known as the Orange Line. By this time, buses had replaced the streetcars that crisscrossed the city. On the left is Alson's Men's Shop which had been founded by Abraham Feinstein in 1918 and operated as a fine men's clothing, haberdashery and hat shop.

In the 1990s, Mattapan Square was celebrating its centennial as a popular shopping destination. Here are seen Hair Spirit, Mattapan Dental, Brother's Deli and Restaurant and the Rainbow Shop. The billboard surmounting the roof proudly proclaims "Our Mattapan. Many Pasts. One Future." As Massachusetts State Representative Dan Cullinane said in 2014, "Mattapan Square is a gateway to the city of Boston" from the south and the two large bronze sculptures *Rise* by Fern Cunningham and Karen Eutemey, have marked that gateway to Boston since 2005.

5

ALONG BLUE HILL AVENUE

The Morton Theatre was at 1163 Blue Hill Avenue and was operated by Boston movie pioneer Jacob Lourie and his partner Sam Pinanski who was later to head the ATC Theaters. Opened in 1926 with 1,308 seats on the main floor and 656 seats in the balcony, the theater had elaborate wall murals and ornate leaded glass panels in the lobby. Saturday Matinees were legendary with twelve cartoons, a serial, news and two movies. By 1943 it was listed as being operated by Paramount Pictures Inc, under the subsidiary Mullins & Pinanski by the Sher Brothers. To the right of the streetcar is the Garber Driving School and Garber Travel Agency, started by Bernie and Beatrice Schwalb Garber, and on the far right Harry's Shoe Repairing. The theater closed in 1966, Garber's moved to Brookline and the entire block was demolished in 1976. Today, it is the location of the Boston Police Department Area B District 3 Mattapan-Dorchester designed by Donham and Sweeney and built in 1987.

The Burt Block was a large wood-framed commercial block with a distinctive corner tower and prominent roof dormers that was built by the Burt Brothers at the corner of Blue Hill Avenue and River Street at the turn of the 20th century. With shops on the ground floor such as a barber shop, creamery and grocery store, it had Donovan's Real Estate office, a major marketer of Mattapan lots and houses at the turn of the 20th century, on the second floor. On the far right is the city of Boston comfort station on the edge of the bridge crossing the Neponset River to Milton.

Streetcar 5205, a Type Four streetcar, is stopped in Mattapan Square in 1938 for a passenger heading toward Egleston Square and traveling along Blue Hill Avenue and Seaver Street. The Burt Block had been demolished by this time and a one-story commercial block built with shops such as Woolworth's, Robert's Beauty Salon, Coolidge Clothing, Cummings and others along the avenue. In the distance can be seen automobiles heading across the bridge built in 1901 spanning the Neponset River and connecting Mattapan and Milton across the Neponset River.

Looking west along Blue Hill Avenue in 1915, the area just past Almont Street is lined with three deckers. This postcard is the epitome of the new "Streetcar Suburb," with both streetcars that connected Mattapan Square and Egleston Square in Roxbury, well paved automobile roads and electrical poles that provided service to the newly built houses. This uniform streetscape of three deckers creates in wood what had been planned for Boston's South End which was built in the 1850s with streetscapes of red brick. Sharing a uniformity of height, setback, building material and similarity of design, early Mattapan in the 1900 to 1925 period saw a tremendous building boom. (Author's collection)

These three deckers, seen in the 1950s, are 1450, on the left, to 1462 Blue Hill Avenue. These four three deckers were designed by R.A. Watson and built as speculative housing in 1909 for developer James Flaherty. They were almost identical is style and design and the two three deckers on the left still retain their shutters, which were not just decorative but could be closed to shield the sun. With ease of transportation, initially by the streetcar whose tracks can be seen in the foreground, and later by bus and the automobile, this was a major reason Mattapan was so built up by the 1940s.

Looking north on Blue Hill Avenue in 1930, the streetcar tracks and overhead wires show not just progress, but the means by which the neighborhood grew, at a nickel a ride on the streetcar. As Bill Kass remembers, the streetcars were all "rattles and squeaks clicking down the tracks." On the left are the Almont Apartments, four twelve unit brick and stone buildings designed by Saul Moffie and built in 1926 between 1451 and 1439 Blue Hill Avenue. Just beyond, with a billboard advertising R.G. Sullivan's quality 7-20-4 cigars surmounting the roof at the corner of Tennis Street, is the National D Store. On the right are a row of three deckers somewhat shaded by trees along the avenue. Today the apartment buildings are known as the Wayne at Blue Hill and the store is Tejeda's Family Market.

Blue Hill Avenue at Fessenden Street had a nine-unit apartment building on the right designed by Samuel S. Levy and built in 1925 for developer Julius Corman. On the left is a one-story commercial block designed by James G. Macdonald and built in 1921 for John H. Patterson. The commercial block had the Mattapan Barber and Hair Dressing Shop and the Wellington Beauty Salon. On the left, behind the stores, is a high style Colonial Revival double swell-bay facade three decker at 8 Fessenden Street which was designed by George H. Greene and built in 1914 for Mary Moonie.

Blue Hill Avenue at Hosmer Street had one-story commercial blocks that were built in the 1920s for shops which provided food and services for the thriving neighborhood. From the left are the Columbia Creamery, that also sold National Ice Cream, The Lunch Shop, with a Croft Ale neon sign, the Frank Chin Chinese Laundry, A. Rubin & Son's Clothing Shop, selling full dress suits, tuxedos and cutaways, and M. Winer Company. Morris Winer had immigrated from Russia and with his son Samuel Winer operated a small store specializing in fresh dairy products in Boston's North End and later in Mattapan as self-service stores, though it continued to focus primarily on dairy and as a delicatessen. In 1928 the Winers established the Elm Farm Foods Company, that would have numerous supermarkets throughout the Boston area and by the 1960s the company was the fifth largest retail food chain in New England. The three decker on the left is 1238 Blue Hill Avenue.

Looking west from Morton Street, the center strip on Blue Hill Avenue had trolley tracks with overhead wires. On the left is a row of stores that were designed by Arthur Rosenstein and built in 1923 for Louis H. Epstein; the commercial block had an elaborate roof parapet with a prominent cartouche along with pinnacles surmounting plinths. These one-story shops were rented to a variety of companies such as the Wellington Paint Company, Morton Sandwich Shop selling Pickwick Ale, the Morton Food Mart, Charlie Lee Chinese Laundry, Hi-Grade Bakery, Ruth's Bakery, a National D Store, Crawford Shades and Morrison and Schiff, which sold out to Hebrew National in 1980, with other small stores on the other side of Landor Road for the next two blocks.

Looking west on Blue Hill Avenue from Deering Road toward Goodale Road is the Mobil Gas Station with its red flying Pagasus sign and gas pumps on the right, the Deering Pharmacy, the Economy Shade and Screen Company, and a Rug and Linoleum Store. The area had both commercial and residential development in the early 20th century with primarily three deckers being built. Today, only two three deckers survive with open lots and the Morning Star Baptist Church which dominates the crest of the avenue.

Looking towards Morton Street along Blue Hill Avenue in the late 1930s, an Egleston Station-bound streetcar and automobiles show how busy the neighborhood had become with numerous shops and stores that created a thriving shopping district. In the center is a three decker at 1172 Blue Hill Avenue, designed by C.A. and F.N. Russell and built in 1908, with the Morton Pharmacy on the ground floor, that still dominates the intersection with a huge billboard advertising Schlitz Beer surmounting the roof; to the left was Waldman's Candies owned by Nathan and Shirley Waldman Silver. On the opposite corner is Ye Olde Brown Jug, with its brown jug neon sign, a very popular Chinese food restaurant opened by Carl Shiffman in 1939 and which he used to proudly say that he sold more Chinese food then any place outside Chinatown. In fact, in the November 7, 1964 edition of *The New Yorker* was a quote "Admirers of Cantonese cooking visiting the Mattapan section of Boston may take refuge in Ye Olde Brown Jug Chinese Restaurant, on the corner of Morton Street and Blue Hill Avenue." Mama Market is now on the site of the Olde Brown Jug.

Blue Hill Avenue was lined with a variety of shops that provided everything one might ever need or want, and all within walking distance of home. A delivery truck is stopped and the shops include Barry's Hobby Shop, Winkler's Bakery, the Morton Lunch Counter which advertises Pickwick Ale, the Morton Public Market, Ruth's Bakery and the Woodrow and Franklin Cafeterias. Nearby was the barber shop of Max Platter and Max Nimoy, the father of Leonard Nimoy, Davidson's Hebrew Book Store and the Blue Hill Bakery. A truck obscures the American Kosher Products which was owned and operated by Harry Weiner, and later his son Leon "Sonny" Weiner as a kosher shop with meat that came from animals that have split hooves, such as cows, sheep, and goats, and which chewed their cud. Elias Katz worked as the mashgiach, the kashrut supervisor, at American Kosher Products for over forty years. Notice the enormous billboard at the Blue Hill Avenue and Morton Street intersection. Today Ali's Roti Restaurant is on the site of American Kosher Products.

The Morton Building, which gently curved around the corner at Blue Hill Avenue and Morton Street was a two-story office building, with the Morton Theatre on the Blue Hill Avenue side, that was designed by Frederick Norcross and built in 1922. Some of the shops were Arlex Auto Driving School founded in 1946 and now the oldest driving school in Massachusetts, Artex Signs, the Meyer Leshgold's Blue Hill Barbershop, Bea Zorn's Dresses, Golden's Cleaners and Tailoring, Anthony's Cleaners and Launderers and the Grove Hall Bank; in the basement was Barney's Pool Hall. On the second floor were numerous credit unions, among them the Blue Hill Credit Union, Mohliver Credit and the Friendship Credit. Notice the large number of billboards including the huge Dawson's Gold Crown Ale billboard, the Mobil gas station on the left with the red flying Pegasus and the tall neon sign of the Morton Theatre. This is often referred to as the traditional boundary line between Dorchester and Mattapan, but in this book I have include the blocks just to the north including Frontenac and Livingston Streets, Woodrow Avenue and Columbine (now Ansel) Road on the right.

Blue Hill Avenue, near Columbine (now Ansel) Street, had one-story commercial blocks designed by Fred A. Norcross on the left and Silverman Engineering Company on the right that had well known stores that were an important part of the neighborhood. From left to right are the Blue Hill Avenue Bakery, Woodrow Cafeteria, Braverman's Men's, Ladies and Children's Wear, a kosher meat market, Garmon's Food Mart (later Prime Market owned by Schwartz and Getman) and the famous G&G Delicatessen, redesigned in 1948 by the Beacon Construction Company for use as a restaurant fondly called "The Greasy Guppel" which was opened by Irving Green and Charley Goldstein. Jim Coleman, Jr. recalled "The G&G to me was like entering a foreign country. Mostly Yiddish was spoken there when I went as a kid." Today Tender Heart Day Care Center, Nu Flav Restaurant, L' Alliance Missionnaire, A Nu Look Salon and the Family Hardware Store are here.

The one-story commercial block seen here was designed by Silverman Engineering Company, founded in 1909 by Peyser and Nathaniel Silverman, and built in 1915 for Benjamin Kopman as a one-story red brick and cement building for small shops on Blue Hill Avenue between Columbine Street (now Ansel Road) and Woodrow Avenue. From left to right are Cohen's Shoes, Lautman's Pizza Shop, Sack's Creamery and Groceries, Woodrow 5 Cent to $1.00 Store and Braverman's Clothing Store. As Scott Miller recalled Blue Hill Avenue "was a vibrant street with any store you needed to buy food, clothes or toys." Out of site was Rosalie's Hosiery Shop and the New Yorker Deli. On the far right can be seen the Fisher Auto Body Shop.

A Type Five car No. 5738 travels north on Blue Hill Avenue, just past Morton Street in 1955. On the left is 1107 Blue Hill Avenue that was designed by Stebbins and Watkins and built in 1907 for developer Joseph Stewart as a three-story red brick and limestone twelve-unit apartment building, Young Israel of Mattapan with its new facade and awning extending to the sidewalk, and 1089 Blue Hill Avenue, a two-family house designed by R.J. Driscoll and built in 1903. On the right is the Prime Super Market, opened by Schwartz and Getman in 1935 with a neon sign designed by Robert Cohen Electric Company, and just out of site on the far right the G&G Delicatessen. On the far left, at the corner of Wilcox Street, was the Rotman Brothers Barbershop called "The Cellar." Notice how many mature trees lined Blue Hill Avenue in the mid-20th century. (Courtesy of Frank Pfuhler)

6

MATTAPAN BUSINESSES

Joseph Lewis, standing second from the left, was a coal dealer in Mattapan, Dorchester and Roxbury and he and his employees would deliver coal to local homes for furnaces by the truckload or in smaller sacks. He also delivered kerosene for kitchen stoves as well as bags of kindling wood as well as blocks of ice for iceboxes. Lewis was a sole proprietor, and was born in Russia in 1913, he was typical of the new immigrants to the United States in working hard and with determination to succeed. The man on the right is pouring kerosene from a tin can into a tin basin and the two boys to his left have a canvas sack of coal and a bag of kindling wood. (Courtesy of Burt Lewis and Family)

In 1923, the G&G Delicatessen opened at 1106 Blue Hill Avenue when Irving Green and Charlie Goldstein became partners at their delicatessen at the corner of Blue Hill Avenue and Columbine Street (later renamed Ansel Road) where it became a popular deli in the Dorchester-Mattapan community. Hillel Levine recalled it as "a place to dine, cut deals, and evaluate prospective sons-in-law." The G&G was also a traditional stop for overstuffed sandwiches of corned beef, pastrami, chopped liver, tongue, kippur, kasha mit varniishkes, cheesecake, handshakes and lively political banter. On election eve, politicians and voters by the thousands flocked to the G&G to be seen and heard from atop the tables and counters as well as, later in the evening, from the kleig-lighted platform traditionally erected beneath the towering red neon sign outside by the old Ward 14 Democratic Committee. Benjamin Klingsberg, who bought the G&G from Irving Green, and whose sandwiches and clientele have been immortalized by dozens of authors and hundreds of politicians, operated the G&G Delicatessen on Blue Hill Avenue from 1952 until it was closed in 1968. Today this is the Family Hardware Store.

Do you remember the action neon sign of a dachshund in a bun wagging its tail? Simco's advertised the World's Largest "old tyme franks" and has become a landmark at 1509 Blue Hill Avenue in Mattapan since it was opened in 1935 by Harry Simberg, a resident of Tennis Road. Simco's "On the Bridge" is Mattapan's contribution to the culinary history of Boston and their hot dogs are still thin, juicy wieners with a barely noticeable skin, which can be served with a variety of traditional toppings or served with cumin-rich beef-bean chili or melted American cheese, but whatever one chooses the hot dog buns are buttered and grilled evoking a sense of continued tradition since its founding. Later owned by Ed Adelson and his son Mendy Adelson, they continued the tradition of serving comfort food; in the 1970s the store was sold to Adelson's brother-in-law Malcolm Krozen. In 2013 Simco's was awarded the Best Hot Dog by Best of Boston, and one customer said that it is "Quintessential throwback boardwalk diner food. If you're after a hot dog that's way too big, giant greasy double cheeseburgers... this is your spot. It's a curbside restaurant with a vintage aesthetic, walk up windows and a huge neon sign." Today, Simco's on the Bridge is owned by Kostas Karampekios.

On the left is a sign for Lipson Fisk Tires and the Pontiac Dealership was at 1299 Blue Hill Avenue at the corner of Wellington Hill Street. Offering both sales of General Motors' *Oakland* line, Pontiac, seen in profile on the neon sign was the brand which was named after Pontiac, Grand Chief of the Ottawa Native Americans, who was famous for his 1763 rebellion against Fort Detroit. This silhouette of Pontiac was used in marketing throughout the early life of the brand. The building later became Jorge Epstein's well known Old Mansions in Mattapan, the legendary architectural salvage business that took up a city block on Blue Hill Avenue. Here one could view room after room of architectural details and fixtures that Epstein, a pioneer in the reuse of architectural details, collected from urban renewal projects throughout the city. Mantle pieces, doors, cornices, columns and metal grates were offered to both professional and amateur restoration projects with a heady aroma of mold and more than a covering of dust. Today this is Frugal Furniture and the Child Care Center.

By the 1920s, Blue Hill Avenue, near Tennis Road, was built up with a variety of housing from single and two-family houses, three deckers and large apartment buildings with many residents commuting to Boston by the streetcar that connected Mattapan with both Egleston Square and Dudley Square. On the left is the National D Store, which was started as a cooperative store by Morris Sanderson of Sanderson's Creamery at 1180 Blue Hill Avenue in Mattapan. He joined other local creamery owners to buy cream, cheese and pickles in bulk which eventually turned into the National D Stores. The chain of small grocery stores offered quality service as well as the convenience of grocery shopping for the neighborhood residents. Later, as part of a regional chain, it could offer savings on canned goods along with polite counter service. First National Stores bought National D Stores during the Great Depression. Notice how heavily built up Blue Hill Avenue was by 1935.

The Jenney Gasoline Service Station was designed by Parsons & Wait and built in 1924 on Morton Street, just west of Blue Hill Avenue. An attractive gasoline station with a clock face in a roundel above the entrance, it had a slate and copper shingled roof and a cupola. With four gas pumps, it was a part of the ascendancy of the automobile in the early 20th century. Jenney was founded in 1812 in South Boston by Stephen Jenney who initially sold kerosene, coal and whale oil, and after 1856 his sons Bernard Jenney and Francis H. Jenney dealt exclusively in the production and distribution of petroleum. Notice the rear of the three deckers in the distance on Deering Road seen above the "Jenney Gasoline" sign in mosaic tile on the right, and the three deckers on the left on Morton Street. Today this is the site of Suds. (Author's collection)

Do you remember the jingle "You can save a pretty penny, buy your gasoline at Jenney. Jenney is so good for your car." The Jenney Gasoline Station seen here was built in 1935 on Blue Hill Avenue near Mattapan Square across from Babson Street. It was said that by the early 20th century the works of Jenney Manufacturing Company in City Point, South Boston had a capacity of 500 barrels of oil a day. Jenney produced auto oil and gasoline and would become a major supplier to automobile owners by the time of 1920; the company was later to be merged into Cities Service in 1965 and the Jenney name was replaced by Citgo. This charming Colonial Revival gasoline station was built of white clapboards and shuttered six over one windows; in the center above the Jenny Gasoline sign is a house on Regis Road. Today, this is the parking lot for the Mattapan Community Health Center. (Author's collection)

John F. Duby, a native of Eastern Townships, Quebec, was an early automotive aficionado, entrepreneur and was entirely self-taught in the trade. He was an early agent for Ford Cars. The Ford Model T Touring automobile was a style of open car without a fixed roof introduced by Henry Ford in 1908 and manufactured at the moving assembly line at Ford's revolutionary Highland Park, Illinois plant. The automobile seated four or more people, and was popular from the early 1900s to the 1920s. Duby's salesroom and garage was at 1348 Blue Hill Avenue and he is seen emerging from the garage seated behind the steering wheel in a Ford Touring car which he offered for sale at $490.00, as well as a less expensive Ford Roadster car at $440.00 thanks to their being mass produced. As he once said, it is "Better to be on the inside looking out than on the outside looking in." His shop also offered Goodrich tires and had gasoline pumps. Today it is the parking lot for the Mattapan Library. (Courtesy of Barbara Duby)

John J. Delaney Chevrolet was founded in 1922 and was referred to as "Boston's oldest Chevrolet dealer." Delaney, who originally lived at 1519 Blue Hill Avenue, started as a used car dealer with an automotive shop on Blue Hill Avenue beside Simco's and created Rexford Finance which according to his granddaughter was like "a precursor to GMAC finance! Redford was the name of the side street near his house at 1537 Blue Hill Avenue." Within a few years he moved across the street to 1590 Blue Hill Avenue and began selling automobiles by Chevrolet which had been founded in 1911 by Arthur and Louis Chevrolet and William Durant in Detroit. In 1917 the company merged with General Motors and in the 1920-1950 period the company competed with Ford, and after the Chrysler Corporation formed Plymouth in 1928, Plymouth, Ford, and Chevrolet were known as the "Low-priced three." Do you remember the song "See the U.S.A. In Your Chevrolet," with lyrics and music by Leo Corday and Leon Carr and sung by Dinah Shore written for the Chevrolet Division of General Motors? Delaney was a successful dealer who generously provided the cars for Milton High School driving education as well as sponsoring the Soap Box Derby. He also had a used car lot near Neponset Circle in Dorchester. (Courtesy of Mary Ellen Carney)

Cote Motor Company was at 926 Cummins Highway where Arthur V. Cote was a New England Ford dealer, as well as owner of Cote Motor Company and Ford Power Products of Boston until 1976. In 1933, Cote Motor Company sponsored Fred Frame in the first stock car race in the United States and he won the race. Arthur Cote also sponsored the local Punt, Pass, and Kick Football contest at the Almont Street Park every fall. Today, Davis Square Architects is currently working on Cote Village, the redevelopment of the former Cote Ford Dealership located on Cummins Highway and Regis Road in Mattapan, as a mixed-use affordable housing development. The project will provide various residential units, as flats and townhouse units, as well as a community room. Cote Village is located next to the Blue Hill Avenue stop on the MBTA Commuter Rail Fairmount Line, which has created ease of transportation for new residents commuting to Boston. (Courtesy of Arthur Cote, Jr.)

Visnik's was at 682-686 Cummins Highway at Itasca Street in a stucco and Spanish tile roof service center. They offered sales and service of Studebaker and Packard automobiles and pumped ESSO gasoline which was founded in 1912 as a service station for the ascendancy of automobiles but became well known through the advertising of Tony the Tiger, which said *Put a Tiger in Your Tank*, which was invented in 1959 by Emery Smith. Started by Benjamin Visnick and later operated by his sons Bernard and Henry Visnik, they sold Studebaker automobiles from a one-room showroom on Cummins Highway in Mattapan. The first automobiles to be manufactured by Studebaker were marketed in 1912 and over the next 50 years, the company established a reputation for quality, durability and reliability. In the early 1960s at the zenith of the Big Three's popularity, it was said to be a statement to drive a Studebaker. Today this is Petro Plus Super Station. (Courtesy of Martin Visnick)

The Modern Auto Parts Company was at 676 Morton Street and owned by Leo Abrahams. The sign advertises "First and Foremost" spark plugs, filters and fuel pumps, as well as parts one might need to service automobiles. On the right is the rear of the Morton Theater at the corner of Blue Hill Avenue and Morton Street, and on the left is a large neon sign for Chez Vous Skating, formerly known as the Morton Arena, which was renamed Chez Vous Rollerway in 1935. Today, Advance Auto Parts and Regal Donuts is located here. (Courtesy of Rebecca Scimone)

The Schlossberg Family has been involved in the funeral business since 1920 when Barney Schlossberg arranged Jewish funerals out of his house in Roxbury. Schlossberg himself built simple wooden caskets while his wife sewed shrouds. He later rented a storefront in Grove Hall for B. Schlossberg and Sons. In the 1930's, B. Schlossberg and Sons moved to 1272 Blue Hill Avenue in Mattapan where in the late 1930's he was joined in the business by his son Louis Schlossberg. After World War II, Louis purchased the business from Barney and, shortly thereafter, was joined by his younger brother Albert Schlossberg. In the early 1950's the Scholossbergs built a free-standing Chapel at 1257 Blue Hill Avenue, a brick colonial building with air conditioning and ample parking. In the early 1970's Louis followed the movement of the Jewish community from Mattapan to the suburbs and purchased the former Trinity Episcopal Church in Canton where they continue to serve the Jewish community of Greater Boston. Today, the site of the Schlossberg-Solomon Chapel is the Morningstar Baptist Church. (Courtesy of Kenneth Schlossberg)

The Grove Hall Savings Bank had a branch at the corner of Morton Street and Blue Hill Avenue. The bank was incorporated in 1914 and was originally in the Silva Building at Grove Hall in Roxbury with Albert A. Ginzberg serving as the president and Samuel A. Singer as vice president. In 1931 a new bank was designed by Krokyn and Browne and built at the corner of Blue Hill Avenue and Georgia Street. By the 1950s the bank had grown tremendously and the Morton Street Branch was opened in a modern glass-windowed office on the ground floor of the rounded corner of the Morton Building. The bank served both the Roxbury and Mattapan neighborhoods until 1969 when it moved to Brighton Center. In 1991 the bank was renamed the Grove Bank and in 1997 it became part of Citizens Bank. (Author's collection)

7

Mattapan Institutions

Children are greeted at the Prendergast Preventorium by Sarah Williams, RN as they arrive with their suitcases in July 1952 for a week of summer camp at the home at 1000 Harvard Street in Mattapan. The preventorium, named for Joseph L. Prendergast who served as president, was established as a lodging place for working men who were not free enough from consumption to sleep in their homes and was developed into quarters for men on the waiting list for a local sanitarium. When it was established, the Prendergast Preventorium was located in the country and it was thought beneficial for tubercular patients with its clean air and sunshine. Later, it was the Boston Tuberculosis Association which would host an annual camp season for inner city children to have a week in the country. After the Preventorium was no longer in use, it was purchased by Combined Jewish Philanthropies. The Preventorium building was later used by the Ledgebrook Home, the orphanage of the Greater Boston Jewish Community until the early 1950s. (Author's collection)

Morton Street, looking towards Selden and West Selden Streets in a photograph from 1930, had the Mattapan Police Station on the left and a row of three deckers on the right. Boston Police Station No. 19 was designed by Harrison H. Atwood and built in 1915 at 872 Morton Street adjacent to the bridge spanning the railroad tracks of the New York, New Haven and Hartford Railroad. The brick and concrete police station had corner quoining, twin bracketing under the overhanging pitched roof and a distinctive entrance with two brick piers supporting a roof flanking the stairs. On the right, just past the wood fence are a row of three deckers, 895 to 915 Morton Street at Evans Street, that were designed by Wendell H. Fraser and built in 1927 for developer Joseph Corman (for whom Corman Road was named) as speculative property. Today, Davis Square Architects has designed Morton Station Village, a forty-unit mixed-income development on the former site of Police Station 19.

As early as 1849 the Mattapan Library Association, founded by Increase S. Smith, served the literary and book borrowing needs of the area. Later, the Mattapan Branch of the Boston Public Library was opened as a small reading room in Oakland Hall in Mattapan Square, and was created a branch of the Boston Public Library in 1923. A new purpose-built branch library was designed by Putnam and Cox and built in 1931 at 10 Hazelton Street in Mattapan as the neighborhood's population had increased tremendously. The library was built of red brick and limestone in a Classical Revival style and had books in both English as well as in Yiddish for the numerous Jewish residents in Mattapan. Today the former library is used by the Mattapan Teen Center of the Boys & Girls Clubs of Boston. In 2009, the current Mattapan Branch Library, designed by William Rawn Associates Architects, was opened at 1350 Blue Hill Avenue.

The Main Building of the City of Boston Consumptives Hospital was designed by Maginnis and Walsh and built in 1915 on River Street for the treatment of patients suffering from consumption. Often referred to as the Boston Sanatorium, the building was part of an extensive campus that was said to be the largest tuberculosis hospital in Massachusetts, and which was built in response to reports that the disease was responsible for more deaths than any other in the city of Boston. The facility was used for the treatment of tuberculosis throughout the 20th century. In 2005, Trinity Foley Ltd. Transformed the building into senior living and adult care through Edwards and Kelcey Architects and is now known as the Foley Senior Residences. The building was listed on the National Register of Historic Places in 2002.